Swing the Light

Nick Collett

Grosvenor House
Publishing Limited

This book is published by
Grosvenor House Publishing Ltd
Link House
140 The Broadway, Tolworth, Surrey, KT6 7HT.
www.grosvenorhousepublishing.co.uk

ISBN 978-1-83975-487-6

Swing the Light and tell me tall tales of the salty sea.

'A friend was in the Navy, and when in the Far East, became drunk in a less than salubrious area of town frequented by transsexuals. He fell asleep lying face up across a table and then, because his T shirt became raised up, his midriff was exposed. One of the transsexual boys planted a large kiss just below his naval painting a large pair of red lips by his lipstick.

His naval colleagues realised that the lipstick would rub off before he woke up. They carried him across to a tattoo parlour and tattooed it in place so he could see it in the morning. He still has it to this day.'

Many thanks to my daughters, Caroline and Katherine, for their assistance creating this book.

My thanks to the County Class Destroyer Association for their help in assisting my memory.

Contents

"To join or not to join"

My parents moved to Lancing in Sussex from Eastbourne so all my friends were then thirty miles away. I worked in a small office as a cost clerk in a commercial vehicle garage. The office was just big enough for three desks and my office colleagues were not far off retirement.

As a nineteen year old this was not very exciting. I was bored and probably feeling a bit lonely. What to do? Was I to drift from one dead end job to another? I had applied for various positions, the RAF[1] and the Hong Kong police force had turned me down. My parents had sent me to the Institute of Industrial Psychology in London to help me decide my future; they said that my talents would be best suited as a Quantity Surveyor. I didn't know what that was.

A good friend of mine had joined the Fleet Air Arm at the age of sixteen and was in the

---

[1] Royal Air force

Far East and apparently enjoying the life. These were the considerations when I made the decision to join the Royal Navy. I made this decision on the top deck of a bus, I remember this moment because I realised that this would be a life changing decision.

Totally nailed it

So off I went to the Brighton recruiting office for a recruitment day. The morning was spent doing tests followed by an interview in the afternoon. At the interview the grizzled Chief Petty Officer[2] at the recruiting centre told me that I had the highest score on the tests that they had ever seen at Brighton. I didn't tell him that was because I had taken the same tests at the Institute of Industrial Psychology and for the Hong Kong police. Each test was taken over eight or ten minutes, an example was a series of diagrams of combinations of triangles of different sizes and orientation to determine whether they matched. My advantage was I knew immediately what the test was about and didn't have to spend valuable seconds understanding the test. It is

---

[2] Recruitment at that time was still carried out by Naval personnel

possible that I had some natural talent as the Institute had told me I had very good visual perception.

What to do?

Given my high test results the Chief told me that with my score I could be anything I liked in the Navy. I declined an offer to be an officer as I could see that as a technical rating was better paid. I chose to be a Radio Mechanician. This was a four year apprenticeship and with one year in school, one year at sea and two more years in school. The apprenticeship specialised in radio, radar, electronics and electrical control systems. A very large part of it, about half, was craftwork in the workshops. Importantly it included a guaranteed promotion path and it paid the most money. Thus, on the 2nd August 1971, I took the train to HMS Raleigh and joined the Royal Navy. So let the salty sea stories begin.

HMS Raleigh

HMS Raleigh was the main basic training centre (and still is). The basic training took six weeks. After two weeks we were sent home on two weeks leave which was very nice. It surprised my parents who thought I had either quit or had been thrown out.

As an apprentice we were paid the same rate as an Able Seaman which doubled my pay compared with my previous earnings as a civilian. In my class there were about thirty of us with an average age of eighteen, the oldest being twenty three, I was 19 at the time. The basic training mainly consisted of drill and marching, use of firearms and a lot of running round the parade ground.

A stab in the arm

It was a requirement to have vaccinations against infections such as yellow fever. We lined up one behind the other, rolled up both our sleeves, took one pace forward and received two injections in one arm from one medic and two in the other arm from another medic. Then we were told to run around the parade ground to pump the injected fluids around our bodies and we all had sore arms for a couple of days. Needless to say, some of the recruits collapsed as a result. One rating went green and fainted at the sight of the needles.

Dangerous sailors

Whilst a lot of time was spent marching and drilling with rifles[3] we also spent a day live firing. The day came when we went to the range. The range was run by two Royal Marines; it struck me at the time that they seemed to be on the edge of a nervous breakdown. I later realised that the unwritten rule is that you do not give sailors firearms and ammunition at the same time unless you want someone to be shot.

Unfortunately, it cannot be determined who that would be. True to form one of our

---

[3] The Navy used the Enfield L1A1 SLR (Self-Loading Rifle)

more intellectually challenged recruits turned from the firing line pointing his rifle at a line of recruits. Whilst we tried to bury ourselves in the ground one of the Marines in charge went berserk and beat him round the head with his beret.

HMS Collingwood

In October of 1971 I was transferred to HMS Collingwood which was the training centre for everything electrical. There were a couple of thousand ratings training at any one time. They were either on fundamental electrical training or were doing familiarisation courses on specific items of equipment.

How many sailors fit in a car

The apprenticeship course did not start until following January so a group of us were kicking our heels for several months. At the time I had a 1952 Austin A30 car.

The A30 is a small car with an acceleration of nought to sixty miles per hour in less than fifteen minutes. My A30 was twenty years old and was difficult to drive. The gear selectors were very worn and the gear lever flopped about with no synchromesh on first gear. The indicators were small, illuminated semaphore arms which were mounted on the door support. These are called Traficators. When selected the arm would rise out of the car to indicate turning left or right, however there were reluctant to return to their start position. I had to open the window and push them back in place to cancel the indication. One of the front headlights would only come on when the driver's door was slammed shut. Unsurprisingly I had several conversations with policemen when out on the road.

On Wednesday and Saturday nights we would often go to the Mecca dance hall in Portsmouth, driving from Fareham (where HMS Collingwood is situated) to Portsmouth. One evening five of us went to the dance hall. With five men in the car it was very squashy with three on the back seat. The A30s back seat is only about four feet wide. There were complaints from my passengers that the car was too small. I told them that we could easily get two more people in the car. When we were leaving the dance hall I was asked whether I was joking about having another two people in the car, I replied "of course not". When I got to the car I found two of my passengers sitting in the back seat with a girl on each lap and the other two were on the front seat sitting on top of one nother.

Changing gear involved a large amount of co-operation from the two front seat passengers. I was surprised the car was even able to move and luckily the police must have been otherwise occupied that night.

Don't insult the ladies

One night, four of us went to Portsmouth. Just outside the dockyard gate there was a line of more than a dozen pubs (Now all demolished). Starting with the Albany the end of the line was the White Swan known as the 'Muddy Duck'. My favourite was the Lenox which consisted of a long, narrow room with a Victorian style bar along one side. Behind the bar the mirrored shelves were full of 'rabbits[4]' brought back by sailors over the last 100 years. As well as sailors it was full of eclectic people such as Big Helen, who had a tattoo above her left knee and liked to tease young sailors.

We started on a pub crawl and eventually arrived at the Muddy Duck which probably built in the nineteenth century. The pub had bare floorboards and the small amount of furniture was nailed down. We

---

[4] Souvenirs – called rabbits because they seem to breed and clutter up the place

went to the bar and as we were about to order our beers to our surprise all the barmen jumped over the substantially built bar. It was all kicking off in a corner of the pub. The barmen evicted the perpetrators and the whole pub went outside to watch the action. Two women proceeded to give a couple of young sailors a good kicking; apparently the ladies had been insulted. After the young sailors had crawled away, we went back into the pub. As far as I can remember this was the only time I saw sailors involved in a fight.

Too much beer?

In the Royal Navy our only expenses were a small daily deduction for food and lodging and we also had to buy our own uniform replacements. During my time in the Navy I was a smoker. There was a monthly cigarette ration of three hundred cigarettes which cost £1. We were paid in cash every fortnight, this meant the remaining money was effectively beer tokens. There was not that much to do on Collingwood in the evenings except go to the bar. At weekends I would drive home and spend most of the time in pubs. I calculated that during my apprenticeship I was drinking sixty pints of beer a week. I tested myself for alcoholism for about four to six weeks in May and June. I stopped drinking during these months as it was the hay fever season. The antihistamine pills had a bad effect when mixed with alcohol.

Wow I was good at that

The apprenticeship consisted of approximately fifty percent in the classroom and fifty percent in the workshops. In the classroom, we learnt electrical and electronic theory and in the workshops, there was a lot of filing blocks of metal by hand. I surprised myself in the workshops because although I had done some metal working at school, I discovered that I was really, really good at it. I could file a block of steel or brass to measurements of accuracy better than a thousandth of an inch. Not only was I able to produce work which marked ninety eight or ninety nine percent but I could do it in half the time taken by my classmates.

When can I be officially sick?

One morning I felt very ill and my colleagues persuaded me that I should go to Sick Bay.

I went to see the medic who took my temperature which turned out to be 105°F. He then told me that I had glandular fever and that I should report to the medical ward. He gave me an A5 piece of card on which was drawn a number of boxes and said that I needed to visit about five different places and collect rubber stamps on the card. HMS Collingwood is spread over more than a square mile so with my high temperature and feeling like death I had to walk to various offices and get this wretched card rubber stamped. When I arrived at the medical Ward the ward medic said to me "oh you should be in bed". Thanks very much, I thought. I got into bed and I slept for three days.

One of the benefits of glandular fever in the Navy is that there was a mandatory grant of two week leave. My instructor was not happy for me to miss that much classroom work so I only got one week. Still one week is better than nothing.

Good food

There was a saying in the Navy "tells lies like a Pussers[5] Menu". This was a real disservice to

---

[5] Slang for Purser

the Navy chefs as they were very good and only limited by the conditions and victuals they were given. Chips[6] were served every day with lunch and dinner. Rumour had it that Captains were more concerned about running out of potatoes than running out of beer. On one ship I was on the potato stock became empty. The chefs valiantly tried to make chips out of instant mash, it didn't work. Luckily the next day we were able to take a load of potatoes on board.

Improved food

In 1973 several hundred Navy caterers and chefs were arrested for corruption. They were getting back handers from suppliers who were providing short measure and low quality produce. When I returned to Collingwood in 1974 the food had improved considerably. In the four dining halls for junior rates, there were over thirty main choices on offer with each dining hall themed to a particular offering.

Navy catering has a certain style and presentation. After I left the Navy I took the family to a holiday camp on Hayling Island where all meals were provided. As soon as I saw

---

[6] Fries (US)

the food offered I realised the camp was staffed by ex Navy chefs.

Navy Tot

The Navy rum tot finished in 1970 so I missed out on it. It consisted of one-eighth of an imperial pint (71 ml) of rum at 95.5 proof which was diluted for junior rates with two parts water. It was then called Grog. Senior rates were provided with their rum without the water. It was served at noon with only fifteen minutes allowed of drinking time. It was a tradition that the glasses used were never washed. A friend of mine acquired one of those glasses which were very encrusted and black with decades of evaporated dark brown rum. He took it home as a souvenir; unfortunately, his mother found it and washed it up much to his chagrin.

A tattoo is forever

That friend was in the Navy, and when in the Far East, became drunk in a less than salubrious area of town frequented by transsexuals. He fell asleep lying face up across a table and then, because his shirt became raised up, his midriff was exposed.

One of the transsexual boys planted a large kiss just below his naval leaving a large pair of red lips painted by the lipstick.

His naval colleagues realised that the lipstick would rub off before he woke up. They carried him across to a tattoo parlour and tattooed it in place so he could see it in the morning. He still has it to this day.'

Old navy sayings

In 1972 my sister was married in Eastbourne town hall registry office. This was one of the few times that I was wearing a full sailor's uniform. We were having photographs taken of the wedding group on the town hall steps. I noticed a little old lady sneaking up behind me so I turned around to confront her. She said, "Touch a sailor's collar for good luck". So I allowed her to touch my collar, I hope it brought her luck. At the time I was not aware of this saying, obviously some clever matelot[7] in the dim and distant past had come up with this really good wheeze for attracting the ladies.

Another saying is "All the nice girls love a sailor" useful for chatting up the ladies. The

---

[7] slang for sailor

fact that a sailor can wash clothes, iron, cook, clean, paint and remove dead wildlife from the premises and stomp spiders all whilst being tremendously romantic all adds to the attraction. In addition, sailors are very good at knots which are useful for those who like adventurous rope work in the bedroom.

There is a response to someone who makes a statement believed to be irrelevant to the conversation. "I have a granny in the Ghurkhas but she is excused boots and gaiters". One meaningless statement deserves another.

My defence your Honour

Since leaving the Navy I've always done the family ironing and so every Saturday morning I would set to, sometimes I would iron twenty shirts and blouses plus other clothes.

I found that doing the ironing has had some side effects, for instance, my wife does not hesitate to purchase difficult to iron clothes such as pleated skirts.

A few years ago, I was going up on an escalator on the London Underground. A couple of steps in front of me, a girl in her twenties was wearing a silk skirt. I found myself thinking 'that skirt could do with an iron', immediately I gave myself a mental kick to remind myself that I was a heterosexual male and I should be admiring her rear not criticising her ironing.

If challenged, when closely examining a woman's clothing which she was currently wearing, I will claim that either I was critiquing the quality of her ironing or admiring her feminine physique. Which explanation I would use would depend on the level of police involvement.

HMS Devonshire

From Collingwood initially I joined an HMS Llandaff[8], which was an ageing frigate and undergoing a major refit at Chatham dockyard. After a few weeks the Ministry of Defence realised that it was not suitable for apprenticeship training and I was drafted to HMS Devonshire.

HMS Devonshire was a County class destroyer. The ship was called a destroyer for

---

[8] Llandaff is a district of Cardiff in Wales – pronounced Clan-daff

but was more like a light cruiser. For political reasons calling her a destroyer made it sound as though it was a smaller and therefore cheaper ship. It was the first County class destroyer to be launched and it was commissioned in 1962, so when I joined it in 1973 it was already showing considerable age.

The concept of the apprenticeship sea training was to work about a month in each department with some electrical associations, otherwise we were the same as any other rating, standing watches (one night in four), painting, cleaning, storing ship etc.

Dry Roasted Master-at-Arms

The Master-at-Arms is the ship's full time policeman. As we sailed into warmer and hotter weather our Master-at-Arms put a notice in Daily Orders[9]. 'Anyone who becomes severely sunburned will be charged with creating a self-inflicted wound' The Master-at-Arms fell asleep that afternoon on the upper deck. I recall seeing a very red

---

[9] Daily Orders – published every day and circulated to the crew. These provide the schedule and activities for the ship.

Master-at-Arms carefully and painfully making his way to sick bay. Spookily enough no mention of self-inflicted wounds was ever heard of again.

Don't sit down!

Whilst in the Caribbean the ship was using of the U.S. Navy live firing ranges. One Saturday we went ashore to an island that the U.S. navy used as a target.(not used as target at the weekends). We anchored offshore off and went by boat to a deserted beach for a banyan[10]. The island was uninhabited and no fishing had been allowed for many years. We arrived at the beautiful unspoilt coral sand beach with large conch shells scattered around and crystal clear sea water. Standing in the sea was like standing in a tropical fish tank. There was thousands of small and brightly coloured fish seemingly unaware of our presence. One of my mess mates had a mask and snorkel and tried to catch a fish in his mask. Unfortunately, during this process, he fell over and sat on a spiky sea urchin. When we stopped laughing we examined the wounds and found that several spikes

---

[10] Banyan - Navy slang for a beach party

had entered his posterior. He was in considerable pain so he went back on board to have the spikes removed by the medic. I was able to borrow his mask and snorkel and swim several metres off the beach. The water was very clear and the visibility was more than five metres. As the island was used as a target by the U.S. Navy I did see a couple of military type four inch shells on the sea bottom mixed in with the sea shells.

A car "borrowed"

We visited Virgin Gorda, part of the British Virgin Islands, for three days. We anchored off and went ashore by boat. I went ashore on my own at about one o'clock and soon found a local shop where I bought myself a bottle of golden Mount Gay rum. I continued to stroll around the island whilst drinking my rum until I came across a bar where five of my messmates were drinking beer. They had hired a Mini Moke[11] to drive around the island. We decided to go for a swim in a remote bay and one of my messmates decided this was a good time to learn to drive. About this time five chefs from the ship up arrived at the bar.

---

[11] A jeep like vehicle based on an Austin Mini

They also thought it was a good idea to go for a swim and asked for a lift. So with myself in the middle of the back seat and my four other mess mates in the car the chefs positioned themselves outside of the car. There was one holding on each side and three were sat on the bonnet. Our learner driver could not actually see where he was going and the plan was that those sitting on the bonnet would shout out "left" or "right" as the case arose. We didn't even make it round the first corner. I heard somebody shout "jump!" and the chefs left us, the car went through a barbed wire fence and down a three foot drop into a field. There was only myself and the driver left in the car, fortunately no one was hurt. The barded wire had wrapped itself around the front wheels rendering the car unmovable.

I got out of the car and walked up the road in search of a replacement. About thirty yards up the road I found a garage with no one about. A Mini Moke was parked inside. I got in and wondered how to hot-wire a car. Whilst considering this I opened the ashtray and there was the ignition key. I started the car and reversed it out of the garage onto the road. By this time the rum was having a distinct effect on my eyes and I was seeing double. My eyes were just not syncing together. The solution to this problem was solved by driving with one eye shut so I would only see one road and not two. I arrived at the scene of the accident and shouted to my messmates, "I've got another car". At this point if I heard a very quiet voice say to me, "Can I have my car back please". I looked to my right and there standing was a local who was very large, well capable of playing as a Full Back. I said "Certainly." And I got out of the car. The local was the garage owner and had walked down the road to see what all the fuss was about. He was very nice about the fact that I had "borrowed" his car and said, "have a good day and be careful". We shook hands and I went back to my messmates. They had untangled the original car from the barbed wire and had manhandled it back onto the road.

Swimming while drunk is not a good idea

We set off for the bay without the chefs who had gone back to the bar. We found the bay and went swimming in the sea where I discovered that swimming whilst drunk is a very bad idea. This is because, when under water, the sense of up and down is lost.

The driver managed to loose the car key. My messmates searched the beach to no avail. I sat in the back of the car and pulled out a bunch of keys which I carried around for no good reason. I probably thought it was fashionable at the time. One of them fitted the ignition and off we went.

My memory fails me at this point, probably due to my rum soaked brain, but I was back on board later that evening. This was followed by a massive two day hangover so I didn't go ashore again.

Virgin Gorda was, in 1973, a sleepy island with a population of approximately nine hundred. HMS Devonshire's complement was four hundred and seventy. I doubt if we were remembered very fondly there, among other things the naval patrol got drunk and were arrested by the island police.

Fort Lauderdale

We arrived in Fort Lauderdale in Florida along with HMS Ark Royal. This was before Fort Lauderdale became the major cruise embarkation port it is today. We were alongside a jetty very close to a major road and we were there for six days. During our time in Fort Lauderdale, we only worked till midday and so after lunch I would set out and hitchhike towards Miami Beach.

Most of the time I was on my own as it was easier to hitchhike, and I found a small bar with a friendly barmaid who provided me with free beer during her afternoon shift. It was very difficult to buy a beer as the locals insisted on buying. While at the bar the local sheriff came in for a bite and bought me a whisky.

'Shouty' Radio Ads

Whilst in Fort Lauderdale the ships entertainment system was tuned to a local radio station. In 1973 the UK didn't have commercial radio (first commercial radio was in October that year). Thus it was that the local radio in the USA had adverts. One advert in particular was very 'shouty[12]'. The advert went something like 'COME DOWN TO FREDS AUTOS FOR THE BEST DEAL WE'VE EVER HAD....' spoken very loudly and very quickly. The same advert was repeated frequently and six months later we could

---

[12] US Presidents are not the only people who can make up words.

recall the complete two minute advert word for word. I'm sure the admen would be proud.

Taff and I try to spend some money

One afternoon, my messmate Taff, a Welshman, and I set out to hitchhike to Miami Beach. We wanted to go to the fancy hotels which had featured in the movies. We stopped by my friendly barmaid's bar and spent a few happy hours there drinking free beer.

We got a lift from the Dean of Miami Cathedral in his big Cadillac to Miami Beach. The Dean dropped us off at the Americana hotel (since demolished). We went inside to a large lobby where there were a number of shops. We must have been looking lost as a woman came out of one of the shops and asked us if we were off the ships. There had been a big PR campaign by the Navy for this show the flag visit, and as we wore uniform, we were easily identifiable. The woman from the shop pointed out the bar and the coffee bar. Taff, who was an excellent actor, hung his head, looked sad and said "We are poor sailors who don't get paid very much. I don't think we can afford them".

He was being somewhat economical with the truth because between us we probably had at least five hundred dollars. However, the woman ran back to her shop came back with her purse and gave us a ten dollar bill. We headed straight for the bar and Taff had a brandy and I had a Scotch whisky.

This was my first visit to the US and I was unfamiliar with the protocol visa vie buying drinks at a bar. Up to this point I hadn't bought a single drink. As is the standard protocol the barman put the bill on the bar between us. After a while the barman took the bill and rang it up. We asked him what was going on and he said that the bill had been paid by a gentleman further down the bar, so we ordered another round. We stayed in the Americana bar until we actually had to pay for a drink which took several hours.

We left the Americana hotel in the evening with the intention of hitchhiking back to the ship but were waylaid at several bars. At about two o'clock in the morning we arrived in a small bar where I talked to a Native American gentleman. He was huge with hands like shovels but very quietly spoken. He had with him a lad of about eighteen years old. Suddenly the bar room door crashed open and there stood a small and diminutive woman. She started screaming at the top of her voice. I could not understand what she was saying. Immediately the lad vanished but the large Native American never moved, flinched or even turned round to look. I asked him who that was; he said in his soft voice, "That was my wife".

After visiting yet another bar where a sailor from the Ark Royal was playing beautifully on a grand piano we watched the dawn come up and we returned on board about six o'clock in the morning.

Taff is abducted

Taff was on duty the day after our run ashore and he was put on gangway guard. After only about an hour sleep and unshaven I saw him leaning against the gangway in the hot Florida sun looking like death warmed up. At around nine o'clock a convertible stopped and two girls got out. One of them ran over to Taff and threw her arms around him. She told him she wanted to take him out for the day. Taff told her go and talk to the man with the gold rings on his arm, this being the officer of the day. She skipped up the gangway and told the officer she wanted to take Taff out for the day. The officer looked at him and said to her in a weary voice "Take him". She went back down the gangway and she and her friend dragged him off into the car. He was returned later that night. If you want to know what happened, then you will have to ask Taff as he was never one to kiss and tell.

Knights of the Sea

During my time in the Navy women were not allowed to go to sea, the WRENs[13] performed similar roles to the men but only on Shore establishments.

The Royal Naval sailors' attitude towards women was to treat them with the utmost respect, chivalry and attention. All women were treated the same way irrespective of their station in life, whether they were a lady of the night or royalty. A sailor may see a lady of the night one day and shake hands with royalty the following day; of course we did wash our hands in between.

Dial-a-sailor

During a Show-the-Flag visit to a friendly country the Navy often ran something called

---

[13] Women's Royal Naval Service

Dial-a- sailor. Advertisements would be placed in local newspapers which stated that if anyone would like to show one of our sailors some of their country and take them out for the day, phone or drop by the ship and they would be issued with a sailor. It was a point of honour that no invitation would be refused although there would not be a choice of a sailor.

There were some potential traps to the Dial-a-sailor scheme. Perhaps a sailor would meet a girl and the pair became very friendly. Sometimes she would find out the next port of call and when the ship arrived, she would be there on the dockside and a good time would be had by all. Eventually the ship would arrive in the home port such as Portsmouth or Plymouth and the girl would be there to meet him. Often at the other end of the jetty would be the wife or fiancé. Much embarrassment all round.

It wasn't all bad, one of my classmates was taken out by a wealthy couple in their fifties when his ship was in California. The couple had no children and followed the ship. They became friends and he invited the couple to his wedding.

Give me the money

Local overseas allowance (LOA) was paid to servicemen serving abroad to compensate for the higher cost of living in the more expensive countries. In 1973 the LOA pretty much doubled my daily pay rate when we were in the Caribbean and North America. Interestingly LOA was paid from the day we touched the first Port to the day we left the last Port to come home including time spent at sea. This meant, by the time we got to Florida, I recall I had over £650 in my locker in cash. The Purser was asking us to lend him money because, obviously, there's only so much cash on a ship. In 1973 my standard Navy pay rate was £4.82 per day worth about £40 today.

Women in the USA

Whilst in Florida I found that American women can be very determined people who set out to get what they want, and what some of them seemed to want was a British sailor. In 1973 it was near the end of the Vietnam War and in the middle of the hippie period. We were unusual in being clean cut and having short hair. The other thing is we had an English accent which for some American women seems to be like catnip. The result of this was that there were a number of affairs which stimulated a certain level of desertion. The US government has traditionally refused to return Royal Navy deserters and in 1973 this still pertained[14]. HMS Ark Royal was with us at the time and I heard they lost seventeen ratings to desertion. If you desert from the Royal Navy they do not give up looking for you until you're eighty years old.

The current 2003 extradition treaty between the USA and the UK states in Article 4, Political and Military Offenses:

4. The competent authority of the Requested State may refuse extradition for offenses under military law that are not offenses under ordinary criminal law. In the United States, the executive branch is the competent authority for the purposes of this Article.

My reading of this agreement is nothing has changed.

Desertion

One of my mess mates met a young lady in Florida and got on very well. When we returned to the UK in the summer he went ashore on leave on the Friday but by Sunday he had run out of money and returned to the

---

[14] One of the causes of the war of 1812

ship. He then found that his lady from Florida had sent him a return air ticket. He did not have the money to buy a train ticket from Portsmouth to Heathrow so I lent him £10 and away he went. In Florida he got engaged to be married but returned to the ship and paid me back the £10. He put in a request to the Navy to get married, as you had to do, which was approved. He went back to Florida at Christmas on leave, got married and never came back. I think I saw him in Typhoon Lagoon in Walt Disney World a couple of years ago, he looked very happy playing in the water with his grandchildren but I did not approach him.

Mugged in Philadelphia

After Fort Lauderdale our next major port of call was Philadelphia. We were moored in the naval dockyards which were about thirty minutes walk from downtown. One evening I was walking back from the centre of Philadelphia, when I heard running footsteps behind me, followed by a sharp pain on my back. I turned around and was astonished to see two teenagers each holding a belt in their hand. One of them had used his belt to lash me across the back.

I was carrying a package which consisted of a pack of giant cigars. The cigars were eight inches long with a diameter of one inch and subsequently I discovered they were terrible smokes.

I presume the teenagers expected me to drop my package and run off. I am six foot three inches and they were only about five foot tall. I asked him what they were doing, they somewhat sheepishly answered that they thought I was an Iranian, I don't know why they thought that. We had a brief discussion, shook hands and went our separate ways.

They were lucky, one of my mess mates was a Navy lightweight boxer of some repute and when he was attacked by four assailants he knocked out all of them. I'm sure the result would have been different if the teenagers had attacked him.

To this day I am very wary of anyone walking behind me too closely. After this incident I always put some emergency money in my sock as sailors never take their socks off no matter what the current activity.

Where are the Casinos?

I gathered from the locals that the place to go was Atlantic City in New Jersey. This was before the casinos had been built but was a well-known seaside resort. I set out and hitchhiked towards Atlantic City, a van stopped carrying some students. The side door opened and I could see they had a huge bucket full of Ice and beer. They asked me where I was going. I replied, "anywhere you're going".

We went to a beach house which was very nice, they had a telescope set up on the beach and we looked at the moon and drank beer. Later that night I set off to hitchhike back to the ship. I was picked up by a student called Tom who informed me that he was visiting the UK later in the summer. I gave him my address and said look me up when you're in the UK, not expecting to ever see him again. However, when I was on leave he contacted me and we spent a couple of weeks sightseeing in London and the south of England.

I went to Philadelphia in Christmas 1973 and stayed for a couple of weeks with him. We have been friends ever since.

What colour is the ship?

Malta is a very nice Island and we were in Grand Harbour which is right beside the main town of Valletta. We were moored on the other side of the harbour from Valletta. Everybody knows Royal Naval ships are painted a light grey colour but this changed one night when we were in Grand Harbour. During the night condensation formed on the steel and a dust storm blew in from the Sahara desert. When we woke up, one side of the ship looked as though it had been painted the colour of sand. The dust had caked onto the steel and it took us all day clean it off.

How to loom

Whilst in Malta I carried out a Naval Patrol. The Navy does not have military police in the same way of the army; each ship has a Master-at-Arms who has one or two side kicks depending on the size of the ship. Thus naval patrols are formed from the ratings on board. As I've mentioned before you do not give sailors firearms and ammunition or even firearms without them, so a Naval Patrol is heavily armed with an arm band with the letters N and P and a old fashioned policemen's whistle. To make your Naval Patrol's look more official we were required to wear boots and gaiters. Our role, there were three of us, was embarkation Patrol.

In order to get from Valletta, across the Harbour, to the ship we would hire small locally manned boats called dgħajsa[15] (we called them Dice-Os) to transport us across the harbour to where the ship was moored. We were to ensure that this happened in a peaceful manner. Later in the evening two sailors were having a very heated argument at the embarkation point and so I stood behind one sailor looking out over the Harbour. As I am tall I am very good at looming. I waited until one of the sailors noticed me and at that point they immediately ceased their argument. I turned to them and said "I hope you've had a good evening" they mumbled something and quietly got into a boat.

The quality of Naples market

We visited Naples and I was able to go and see Pompeii one hot dry day. I was keen to try genuine Italian food. I and the NAAFI[16] assistant went ashore and found a small local

---

[15] I don't know how to pronounce it either

[16] Navy, Army, and Air Force Institutes: an organization providing canteens, shops, to military personel

restaurant which had pink mirrors, fluorescent lights, Formica tables and a lino floor. Neither of us spoke any Italian and none of the restaurant staff spoke English so we picked from the menu with a pin and had a really wonderful meal.

One of my messmates found a local market with a stall selling electrical goods. There was a transistor radio on display and after some haggling with the vendor he bought the transistor radio. The vendor put the radio into its box but when my mate got back on board he discovered that the box contained nothing other than a brick.

Smelly Toulon

After a NATO exercise we went to Toulon[17] in France. Toulon is one of the main French naval bases in the Mediterranean. The French Navy laid on a tour and a number of us got on a bus with a French driver. The driver spoke no English but we did have a lieutenant who had some schoolboy French. We were unable to determine where we were going so it was

---

[17] In 1793 the British supported Royalist forces against the French revolutionaries and occupied Toulon for four months.

a mystery tour. The bus set off and we went to Nice where we had a look round and we had lunch in a small restaurant. Having had some experience of France I ordered the Plat-du-jour[18] but everyone else ordered burger and chips. When my Plat-du-jour arrived it was much better than the burger and chips.

On our way back to the ship we stopped at a perfume factory where we had a guided tour. The Gift Shop had large amounts of samples which of course we smeared these all over our hands and arms. When we got back to the ship, the powerful perfume we exuded had our mess mates believing we had been in a brothel.

They do that in the Hagia Sofia?

In Istanbul I wanted to see the Hagia Sofia[19], so a group of us got in a taxi with the intention of visiting this famous site. We gave instructions to the driver who took us about four yards to a brothel. This was not where we wanted to go so we got into another taxi and tried again. We were taken to another brothel. This time

_____

[18] Plate of the day
[19] built as a Christian church in the 6th century CE (532–537)

we decided we'd give it a look and so we went in and met some attractive ladies who were offering personal services. A number of my messmates partook of those services whilst the rest of us waited, I would emphasize that I did not indulge. This was a good thing as a few days later a couple of our group had to go to the special clinic[20]. We never got to see the Hagia Sofia and I would still like to visit it.

Life in a blue suit

Life on board was not particularly comfortable, in our mess there were forty eight of us. Bunks were three high on each bulkhead[21]. During the day bedding was zipped up in heavy plastic bags, The middle bank folded down such that a padded bench was created with the lowest bunk. Below the bottom bunk wire racks could hold Navy issue suitcases. Each rating had a locker which was about thirty inches wide, forty inches high and twenty four inches deep. There was also some small amount of hanging space. On the front of the locker was a short rail on which a towel could

---

[20] Clinic for venereal disease
[21] Wall normally made of steel

be hung. We had very little space to store clothes and other items.

There was a wash room with toilets, sinks, and showers. There was no shortage of hot water as it was a steam driven ship but the showers had no thermostat controls. In order to ensure that another shower user was not scolded due to pressure change there were a series of unofficial edicts which were obliged to be shouted in the shower. Before switching the on the shower a shout "switching on" would be made, if at any time an adjustment was to be made to the shower controls a shout "adjusting" and before finishing in the shower a shout of "switching off". Failure to do these simple things would generate a hard time from the other shower users.

The toilet flush was powered by the fire main. The fire main was a supply of seawater constantly pumped round the ship for the fire hoses in the event of fire. The fire main was maintained at a constant pressure of one hundred and fifty pounds per square inch. To flush the toilet a spring lever was pulled which created what seemed to be a small explosion in the pan as the high pressure water forced the pan contents down the pipe. Needless to say there were never any blockages in the sewer pipes. The sewer pipes went straight into the sea, no processing in those days.

The ship had a laundry which was operated by Hong Kong Chinese so we were able to launder our clothes for a fee. Underwear and socks we washed by hand ourselves. At the end of each day, we would have a shower and change into evening uniform before the evening meal. Occasionally we had a Chinese Tailor on board to sew-on badges and repair uniforms.

Junior rates were allowed three cans of beer a day. Other entertainment was limited to a CCTV system where TV programmes would be shown. Films were shown in the junior rates' dining room. The films were selected by a Chief Petty Officer[22] who thought that films such as "Waterloo" and "Charge of the Light Brigade" were suitable for sailors much to our disgust as we would have preferred Bond movies and the like.

In the 1970s there were no mobile phones and no internet. Communication with home was by mail although in emergency a phone call could be made by radio but it was very expensive. Mail was sent to the ports we

---

[22] Equivalent rank to Sergeant Major

visited and occasionally the RAF[23] dropped mail into the sea in a sealed container. On one occasion the RAF made a drop of mail which sank. This turned out to be a 'joke' and the drop did not contain any mail.

Someone feels sick

As previously mentioned, bunks were three high and separated from the opposite set of bunks by three feet. We packed in quite close together. One night a rating that had had a good run ashore[24] was asleep on the bottom bunk. He then produced projectile vomit with such power that it hit the deck head[25]. The result was that five other ratings were spattered with sick. The rating that vomited had to pay for the cleaning of the bedding for everyone affected.

Cat versus sailor

Every evening the mess was cleaned ready for the duty officer to conduct his rounds and inspect the mess. At the end of the night at about 10 o'clock the duty men would collect

---

[23] Royal Air Force
[24] A night out on land
[25] Deck head - ceiling

the gash[26] and if at sea this was dropped overboard at the stern of the ship.

When in Portsmouth Harbour the gash was tossed into a skip on the jetty. The Dockyard was poorly lit and when the gash bag was thrown into the skip a dozen feral cats would jump out. The cats would have been chowing down on the waste food thrown away by the chefs.

The dockyard in Portsmouth has a twenty foot high wall surrounding it. The cats had been introduced into the Dockyard during the age of sail to put down mice and rats. The current cats were their direct descendants as due to the wall they had no means of interacting with cats outside of the Dockyard.

Blackbeard returns

Occasionally we would have groups of children come on board for a visit. Ratings would be detailed to show them round the ship and the ratings would dress up as Pirates. One of my messmates was bigger than me, a very large man who had grown a big black bushy beard. The group of children were being

---

[26] Rubbish

shown around the ship when this sailor appeared dressed as a pirate. Unfortunately, the children thought that he was Blackbeard reincarnated. The kids screamed and ran away. Our pseudo Blackbeard was ordered to stay out of sight so as not to frighten the children.

Flying under water

Following one exercise we had a number of RAF officers on board and as we were going else where, other than a port, we were to transfer them to an RFA[27] by Heaving Line transfer. A Heaving Line transfer consists of a thick rope which was secured to the RFA and onboard our ship it was taken around a big pulley with the rope held by a line of a dozen seamen looking rather like a tug of war. With both ships travelling at speed the seamen could take up the slack or let out the rope as both ships rolled. This ensured the transfer rope was kept out of the water and the correct tension maintained. Attached to the transfer rope was a bosun's chair on a pulley, which looked like a child's swing. The chair

---

[27] Royal Fleet Auxiliary – a supply ship to the Royal Navy

would be pulled across to the RFA by a different rope. One of the RAF officers looked at this system and complained that it looked far too dangerous. To demonstrate we were in control of the situation a rating was volunteered to demonstrate the process. He was successfully transferred to the RFA and back again whilst remaining dry. The RAF officers were convinced and transferred one by one. The complaining RAF officer was the last one to go across and the sailors deliberately slacked off the transfer rope so that he was towed through the water. A nice 'joke' returned.

HMS Collingwood

In January 1974 I returned to HMS Collingwood to complete the final part of my apprenticeship.

The lucrative Coffee Boat

Four of my messmates and I decided to operate a 'Coffee Boat'. We clubbed together some cash and bought an electric kettle, instant coffee, sugar and powered milk so we could have coffee in our mess. When we first plugged in the kettle the heating element exploded, blowing off the stainless steel lid and leaving several dents in the lid where it had impacted the handle. We had forgotten to put any water in it!

After the initial cost we agreed to put some money into a kitty every week to replenish our stacks of the consumables. It became known within our accommodation block that we had cash available and some of the more spendthrift members approached us desiring a loan. We decided to charge 10% interest on loans mainly to discourage borrowers. We were paid in cash every two weeks and the loans were normally requested a day or two before payday. Repayment was due, including the 10%, on payday. Our payday loan operation was very lucrative more by accident than design. We were not really keen to make loans as it was extremely illegal and if discovered by the Navy authorities we would have been deep in the brown and smelly.

After six months we no longer had to put money into the kitty as our payday loan operation fully funded the Coffee Boat. When our apprenticeship came to end we drank the remaining funds on several pub crawls.

Schools out

Whilst my classroom work scores were average my workshop scores were excellent, and I ended up with a credit pass. On completion of my apprenticeship in October 1975 I was promoted to Leading Hand[28].

I then had to wait several months to be drafted to a ship. During this time I was given the job of security driver on HMS Collingwood.

---

[28] Equivalent to the Army rank of Corporal

The role required us (there were two of us on watch) to drive a Navy minivan for six miles around the establishment every hour from six pm to six am. It was a mind-numbing role but had the benefit of three nights on and four nights off. The only excitement was that at seven o'clock each evening we had to check all the safes on site; another tedious task.

Knife fight thwarted

As we had an official vehicle we were the go-to men if the Duty Officer required a speedy response to an incident on the establishment. One evening I was called to the main gate. The main gate is similar to an Army guard room and contained a couple of offices and a cell. The Duty Officer informed me that a soldier, who was on a technical course in HMS Collingwood, had been threatening sailors with a knife in the junior rates bar. The information was that the soldier had now returned to his accommodation block. The officer told me to go and fetch him and bring him back to the main gate. He pointed to the Navy Patrol and said I should take them with me. I turned and looked at the Naval Patrol. It consisted of three sixteen year olds who, with all of them on a weighing machine would have had trouble tipping it over twenty stone (two hundred and eighty pounds). As usual they were each heavily armed with a whistle and an armband. I told my Navy Patrol to get in the back of the van and we went off to find the soldier. I did notice that my Navy Patrol were not keen to take on a knife wielding soldier. I realised that I was going to have to do this on my own. We found the soldiers mess and luckily for me the soldier was sitting on his bed looking somewhat subdued. He had realised that he was in the manure up to his neck and surrendered to us. I asked him where the knife was and he indicated it on his bedside table. I took charge of the knife we all got back in the van and returned to the main gate. I was very relieved not to have been involved in a knife fight.

Revenge of the Rabbit

The Captain on HMS Collingwood had a four bedroom house on site where he lived with his family. One of the family pets was a rabbit and one night the rabbit made a bold attempt to escape. It was found by a steward hopping about outside the Wardroom[29]. The steward took it back to his accommodation and put the rabbit in his locker. (In Collingwood the "locker" was the size of a wardrobe so the rabbit was in no great danger). The steward went to the junior ratings bar and told a number of people he had a new pet. Someone in the bar realised that this was the missing Captain's rabbit and it was reported to the Duty Officer.

I was called to the main gate and ordered along with the requisite Navy Patrol go to the accommodation block and recover the rabbit. I found the steward who was holding the rabbit but refused to give up the animal. I convinced him to get in the van with the rabbit and go to the main gate and resolve the issue.

When we got to the main gate the steward and rabbit went into the office. The Duty Officer and the Duty Petty Officer[30] tried to convince the steward to give up the rabbit. The Petty Officer was experienced in dealing with ratings and had almost persuaded the steward to give up the

---

[29] Officers Mess
[30] Rank equivalent to Sergeant

rabbit when the Officer of the day lost his temper. He told me and the Navy Patrol to seize the steward and recover the rabbit. We all looked at one another and then pounced. Three of us jumped the steward and the Petty Officer seized the rabbit which was unharmed during the affray. We put the steward in the cell.

The steward's right arm had a plaster cast and he unravelled the muslin tape which help the plaster together, tied one end to the light fitting, stood on the bed and tied other end round his neck. He demanded the return of the rabbit or he would jump. After a brief conference outside the cell it was decided to rush him. We all rushed in and he jumped off the bed. The muslin, which had no strength, immediately broke. He was then restrained by strapping him into a Neil Robertson stretcher[31], this was a technique the Navy used when dealing with ratings that might harm themselves or otherwise used as a restraint.

The Duty Officer and I took the rabbit to the Captain's house. The Captain's wife answered the door and the officer handed

---

[31] Neil Robertson Stretchers are used for the recovery of patients in difficult emergency situations

her the rabbit. She cooed over the rabbit saying, "you naughty, naughty rabbit". Little did she know the amount of aggravation caused by that rabbit.

The next day the steward appeared at Captain's Table where he was charged. He was sentenced to ninety days in the Navy jail. For my part it was a bit annoying because I had to stay awake during the morning, having been awake all night, but I did feel sorry for the steward.

Summary Justice

For minor offences, such as 'Absent from Place of Duty', the Navy operates summary justice. This takes place at the Captains Table. Either the Captain or the First Lieutenant is the judge at a Captains Table. The charge is brought by the Master-at-Arms or the Regulating Petty Officer and the ratings Divisional Officer speaks for the rating. Sentences could include loss of pay, leave, and work detail or up to ninety days in the short term Navy Prison.

I learnt a lot about summary justice from the wrong side of the table and caused my interest in the law. This may be why I am a lay Magistrate i.e. unpaid.

Prison in the Navy

Serious offenders in the Navy could be sentenced by the Captain to a Navy prison. Sentences handed out would be thirty, sixty or a maximum of ninety days. For any offence which may carry a sentence of more than ninety days a court martial was required.

The concept of the short term Navy prison was to make ratings not want to return. They were controlled every minute of the day with no free time and effectively were held in solitary confinement. The object was to convince ratings that this was hell on earth so they would not want another sentence.

HMS Mermaid

HMS Mermaid was originally built for Ghana. It was to have been named Black Star and to have functioned as the flagship of Ghana's navy as well as the presidential yacht for Kwame Nkrumah, the President of Ghana. He was deposed and the order cancelled. Mermaid was completed in 1968 and in 1971 was bought by the Royal Navy.

A fake warship

HMS Mermaid was an odd ship with one twin gun turret and three Bofors guns. The guns in the turret were date stamped 1944 and both they and the Bofors guns were found to be a danger to the operators and were never fired. The ship had been built primarily to operate in a tropical climate. One of the three engine spaces was full of air conditioning units. Originally there was to be a large presidential launch carried on one side of the ship. In order that ship would be balanced counterweights had been placed in the on the other side to prevent a list. We didn't have the presidential launch and this meant that the ship had a continuous list to starboard.

I joined HMS Mermaid in February 1976 after it had returned from spending 2 years as the Hong Kong guard ship. During its time as a guard ship the air conditioning had been well maintained. However, we were scheduled to go "up the ice[32]" and become involved in the Cod War. Iceland is very cold in February but the fact that Mermaid was built for the tropics did not concern the Admiralty. Today very few people have even heard of the Cod wars.

---

[32] Slang for going to Arctic regions

I Spy a Honey Trap

Before joining HMS Mermaid, I did a course on encryption systems, which all Royal Navy ships carried at the time. One of those systems received coded messages from the Admiralty, decoded the message within the encryption machine, and printed it out on a teleprinter. The encryption machine occasionally required re-syncing based on an accurate time. To do this I used, with great irony, a Russian made digital red LED watch. It was one of the first digital watches manufactured and predated the later LCD watches which became very popular. So I was using a Russian made watch to control an encryption machine designed to prevent foreign powers such as Russia from reading the messages.

During the encryption course we had an hour's presentation from someone connected with spook central. He showed us some fuzzy black and white Polaroid pictures that were claimed to have been used in a Honey Trap style of blackmail. A Honey Trap is where pictures are taken of someone, with knowledge of official secrets, in a compromising situation. The general consensus within the class was that on receipt of such pictures we would ask the sender if the event could be restaged. However on the retake eight by ten inch colour glossy pictures would be required. This was generally the attitude within the Navy which was probably why spies did not bother us, although we would have been very pleased to play our part in a Honey Trap.

Fish? I hate fish

The Cod War was a dispute over fishing between Iceland and the United Kingdom. The Icelanders claimed fishing rights of a two hundred mile limit from their coast. The UK government disagreed with this claim. To enforce this claim the Icelanders used converted trawlers with a reinforced hull. The Icelandic trawler would tow a hook on the end of a long steel cable; the inside of the curve of the hook was sharpened like a knife. When the Icelanders spotted a trawler fishing in the disputed waters they would sail across the stern. The hook would catch in the cables holding the fishing net and cut them. Thus, the British trawler would lose a very expensive fishing net. The role of the Navy was to prevent this by placing a warship in the way of the Icelandic trawler. As a result, depending on how the negotiations were going in London, the Icelanders would ram the warships.

The Icelanders had a point. Earlier in the century cod could be caught over twenty five feet long. (Cod grow continuously) In the 1970s cod could be caught up to six feet long. A trawler gave us two cod which were six feet long. These were sufficient to provide two hundred men with cod steaks, except for me because ironically I hate fish.

"Up the Ice" we go

In March, after overhauling the ship systems especially the heating elements and a work up training off Portland, we went "up the ice". The sea off Iceland in March can be extremely rough; needless to say we went through several major storms. Unusually for a modern warship there was, just aft of the bridge, a large empty room was originally to be the Ghanaian president's stateroom. This had windows along both sides so we were able to see out quite easily when off watch. Frequently on that first trip we had waves of between sixty to eighty feet and Mermaid was a ship of two thousand three hundred tonnes. To provide a comparison, a modern cruise ship such as Cunard's Queen Elizabeth

59

is over ninety thousand tonnes. We bounced around like a cork in a toddler's bath. The ship would travel up one side of the wave and when it went over the top and down the other side the propellers would come out of the water and the engines would race. Our mess was right above the propellers and as they came out of the water they would slam that the sea against the hull with a loud repetitive banging noise.

We defy gravity

When a ship is pushed up by a wave weight apparently increases and it feels heavy and when it goes down it feels that weight has decreased. Galileo proved that objects of different sizes fall at the same rate so when falling we experience weightlessness. Early one morning, when most of the troops were still in their bunks, the stern of the ship must have been pushed down. The result was that everyone floated above their bunks. At the same time the ship gave a lurch sideways moving the bunks from underneath the gravity defying sailors. Gravity then returned and they crashed to the deck in big heaps, lockers came open and chaos reigned. Luckily for me the lurch of the ship meant that I slammed into the bulkhead beside my bunk.

Mouldy ship

The conditions in our mess were cold and damp. Beneath the deck in our mess there was a cold water tank and we had little insulation in the floor. The deck in our mess continually ran with water from condensation, the bedding in the lower bunks became covered in mould. Ratings would slide into their bunks without disturbing the mould.

The food was also affected. We had to scrape blue mould off the slices of bread before eating. However, I would give full marks to the chefs who prepared meals in appalling conditions with the ship rolling and pitching.

On the first trip we were "up the ice" for four weeks and I was seasick for the first two, after which I was fine. The Navy provided some very powerful sea sick pills although these had a strong soporific effect. As soon as I walked on land my sea legs reset and in rough weather I would start two more weeks of seasickness. We had one rating that had not been to sea before and his seasickness was so bad the medic made him unconscious with an injection.

Hold on!

In the dining room each table had a plastic mat in front of each man; these mats had the ability to stop plates from sliding across the table. However the ship rolled so much that we learned to eat whilst holding either the knife or the fork on the plate to stop it sliding across the table. In the evening a film show would be shown in the junior rates dining room. Sometimes it required three ratings to hold the projector to stop it falling over.

Nimble Mermaid

HMS Mermaid was a frigate in name only; a regular Royal Navy frigate has to have sufficient speed to keep up with an aircraft carrier. They could therefore achieve over thirty knots (about thirty five miles per hour). Seeing one of these frigates apply full power was like watching a speed boat taking off with a massive plume of water coming from the stern. Whilst able to do a very high speed, going from forward to reverse took some considerable time. Icelandic trawlers were more nimble. HMS Mermaid being a diesel powered ship had a maximum speed of twenty one knots. There were eight engines connected to two propellers via shafts. Unlike other warships it did have variable pitch propellers; the propeller pitch could be controlled directly from the bridge using a pair of small levers and the ship could almost instantly change from forward to reverse. This made the ship very manoeuvrable.

Trophy of war

In order to counter the Icelanders a fender was rigged consisting of a twenty five foot very heavy timber of about nine inches in diameter. This was threaded through old rubber tyres. During one confrontation an Icelandic trawler attempted to ram us and due to the sea rolling the ships, during the contact, pulled down the fender, broke the rope and the fender fell onto the deck of the trawler. This was no doubt taken away as a trophy of war.

I do hope the Icelanders disposed of the tyres in responsible manner and didn't throw them in the sea.

My most reckless decision

After our second trip "up the ice" I came home on leave. I had been engaged for about a year and on the 1st of April my fiancée asked:

"When are we going to get married?"

I looked at the ships schedule and saw that the plan was to return from Iceland on 21st of May. So I said:

"We could get married on the 22nd of May".

This was a somewhat inconsiderate decision as it left my fiancée and her parents to organise a wedding on their own. It was reckless because there was no guarantee that we would be able to return on 21st of May. So after leave was over, we went back "up the ice".

The importance of six inches

As the weather was better and our trawlers were able to do more fishing, so the Icelanders became more aggressive and more collisions took place with our warships. During these confrontations we would be closed up to Action Stations during which I was based in the Operations room.

For those of you who remember Star Trek, James T Kirk, after an action, would press a button and say:

"What's the damage Scotty?"

My role was similar to Scotty in that I collated damage to the ship so as to able to inform the captain and others. During one confrontation we are rammed and a hole was made in the side of the ship. Beside me in the operations room was a lieutenant who was providing a running commentary to the Admiralty in Whitehall via radio. The lieutenant requested on behalf of the Admiralty 'how deep was the water in the affected compartment'. I contacted Damage Control HQ and asked the question. The reply was that everyone from HQ and had gone to see the compartment with the hole. I grabbed hold of a passing rating and told him to go to the compartment and find out the depth of the water.

Access to the compartment was down a ladder to a small ante room. There was a door which opened into the compartment. The rating returned and told me he could not see into the compartment because there were so many people in the way. However, he did tell me that the water was coming over the coaming at the bottom of the door. This was an ordinary door (not watertight) set in to the steel bulkhead but it had a six inch high coaming at the bottom of the door. I was familiar with this coaming as it had frequently cracked me on the shins and I knew that it was about six inches high. I turned to the lieutenant in the operations room and said:

"There are 6 inches of water in the compartment sir".

This was immediately relayed to the Admiralty. After a few minutes I thought about this and realised the ship stationary was rolling from side to side. Six inches of water in an area of twenty square metres is a lot of water. However, if you tilt the room by twenty degrees there is a lot less and it was likely the water seen was simply slopping over the coaming.

After about an hour during which the ships crew tried and failed to fix a steel plate over the hole on the outside of the ship, the captain made an announcement.

"As we have had six inches of water in the radar power compartment the Admiralty has ordered us to return to Chatham dockyard".

Later that evening I talked to some of the ratings who had been involved and asked them 'how deep was the water?' They have been mopping up the water with cloths; there never had been six inches of water in that compartment at any time. When we arrived back at Chatham the local newspaper printed a photograph of the ship and stated that we had returned to Chatham because we had had six inches of water in a compartment.

I learnt from this that if you put a number on something it will stick like Super Glue. The main benefit from my point of view was that we returned to the Dockyard on the sixteenth of May which allowed me to guarantee my attendance at my own wedding. No doubt to the great relief of my fiancée and her parents. As a result I have been married to my long suffering wife who has put up with me all these years.

It's a wonderful wife

My wife comes from Yorkshire. As such she is very thrifty and pragmatic, so when a few years ago go I was diagnosed with cancer she devised a plan. She has discovered cremations in Florida are a lot cheaper than in the UK. She intends to ship me to Florida, cremate me and then take a cruise back to the UK. She is very fond of cruises and during her trip back from Florida will cast me over the side of the ship. Hopefully by that time I will be dead. She then plans to buy a big memorial stone in my honour, possibly a diamond but most likely an Emerald.

The Theory of Believable Numbers

This issue of the six inches as previously described was one of the things which made me work out the Theory of Believable Numbers. This is where are a verbally stated number is consciously or subconsciously accepted or rejected based on the number itself.

Here is an example, say John goes to an event and afterwards Steve who has not attended the event asked John:

"How many people were at the event".

If John says there were fifty Steve is likely to assume the number given is a guess and that there was anything from forty to sixty people present. If John says:

"There were fifty three people there"

Steve will assume that is a completely accurate figure and that John has either counted all the people or obtained a number from the event organiser.

If someone states a number such as one hundred, five hundred or seven hundred this will be assumed to be an estimate. If the number is ninety seven, five hundred and twenty three or seven hundred and two it will be assumed to be an accurate number. Prime numbers are very effective or giving percentages with at least one decimal point. Even though it's a complete guess it is likely to be believed.

This is not always the case, when the Prime minister says that weapons of mass destruction can be launched in forty five minutes no one seemed to question the number forty five. What was this number based on, who measured it, why is it forty five minutes and not, for example, forty seven minutes.

In 1944 the Germans were able to setup and launch, on a temporary launch site, a V2 rocket, so why in 2002, would it take forty five minutes. Am I an old cynic or is there a reader who can tell me why it was forty five minutes.

Disaster!

We now come to the saddest part of this narrative, which I have found the most difficult to write.

One afternoon I was dozing on my bunk when I heard a loud grinding sound which ran along the side of the ship. Given my experience from our collisions off Iceland I knew immediately that the ship had come in contact with something.

At this time I was living in a mess deck just below the Operations Room. I sprang off my bunk and started rapidly climbing the ladder to the Operations Room. Whilst I was on the ladder, the klaxons sounded and an 'emergency stations' broadcast was made. When I arrived in the Operations Room no one was there and it only took two or three steps for me to go out onto the deck on the starboard side. I was shocked to see a minesweeper upside down with one of its propellers still spinning. There are a lot of men in the sea most of them wearing life jackets. I was stunned and my first thought "What kind of exercise is this" before realising the enormity of what had happened. A rating was trying to launch one of our inflatable life rafts so I went to his aid and we launched four life rafts.

What had happened? We were in the North Sea on a sunny September day with calm seas. The plan was to rendezvous with six minesweepers that had been on an exercise. Mermaid was to escort the minesweepers to Hamburg for a couple of days of R&R.

When we met the minesweepers Rear Admiral Hollins, Admiral Commanding Reserves, who was on board Mermaid, ordered a Heaving Line Transfer. HMS Fittleton was first up. In this case the exercise consisted of the ships steaming alongside each other whilst a sailor from the Fittleton threw a rope across to HMS mermaid. When you have two ships steaming alongside each other there is a venturi effect, this venturi effect sucked the Fittleton against the Port side of the Mermaid. On contact both ships tried to solve the situation. Mermaid changed the engines to full astern whilst the Fittleton tried to pull away. The effect of these was the Fittleton was dragged along the side of Mermaid to the Bows. Mermaid ended up pushing Fittleton sideways and rolled her over.

I have visited the National Archives in Kew to see the files on this disaster. My memory seems to differ from the accounts I found.

HMS Fittleton is in the foreground upside down with HMS Mermaid the larger ship behind. The life rafts I launched can be seen on the right. (Picture taken from a video)

Very quickly Mermaid put a boat in the water and rescued those who were in the sea. Thirty two survivors were rescued with ten ratings missing. Within about tens minutes our ships diver was dressed in a wetsuit, went to Fittleton and climbed on to the upturned hull. He returned to Mermaid and reported that he believed there were ratings still alive within the ship as he could hear tapping from inside. Within a very short time a sleek modern German destroyer appeared and had a boat in the water with four clearance divers on board.

Neither our ships diver nor the clearance divers[33] were allowed to enter the Fittleton. Why was this decision taken? The official reason was the Fittleton could sink at any time taking any divers down with her. However, the Fittleton took a long time to sink. A survivor escaped twenty minutes after the collision. The divers were ready to take the risk but were prevented by order of Admiral Hollis.

Later that evening a rumour spread on board the Mermaid that the Admiral was

---

[33] A ships diver has completed a diving course but has another main role. A clearance diver is a full time diver.

concerned about any diver changing settings on the Fittleton. This rumour caused several ratings to start talking about confronting the Admiral in his cabin and I had to talk them out of this course of action as I knew it would not end well.

The Fittleton was salvaged and taken to Holland to be pumped out. Five dead bodies were discovered within the ship. It is believed that three of them survived for at least forty five minutes inside.

Lieutenant Commander Paget, the captain of the Fittleton, was court martialed and found guilty of negligence. He appealed the verdict which was overturned.

"The Board has concluded that, while Lt Cdr Paget hazarded HMS FITTLETON due to errors of judgment, this did not amount to negligence under Section 19 of the Naval Discipline Act. In these circumstances, the Admiralty Board of the Defence Council has decided that the conviction on Charge 3 is unsafe and unsatisfactory and has accordingly quashed the conviction and annulled the sentence[34]."

HMS Fittleton was manned by the RNVR[35] and most of the men on board came from

---

[34] Official statement to the appeal.
[35] RNVR – Royal Naval Voluntary Reserve

East Sussex where I was born and raised. Members of the RNVR are volunteers who are part time and every year spend two weeks at sea but otherwise have civilian jobs.

Ten lives were lost in this disaster, the worst since WW2. Who is to blame? It appears that a series of errors were made. The Fittleton was not ready for the manoeuvre and came too close to the Mermaid. The Fittleton was at risk due to its small size relative to the Mermaid and should not have been ordered to carry out the Line Transfer.

Medal awarded

ROYAL NAVY COOK AWARDED QUEEN'S GALLANTRY MEDAL[36]

The Queen's Gallantry Medal has been awarded to Leading Cook (SM) David John Young, 27, for saving the life of one rating and contributing to the escape of two others when the minesweeper HMS Fittleton capsized following the collision with the frigate HMS Mermaid on 20 September 1976. At the time of the incident, which occurred off the Dutch coast following a NATO exercise, L/Ck Young was on loan to HMS Fittleton from

---

[36] Taken from a Ministry of Defence News Release

the nuclear powered Fleet Submarine HMS Superb, in which he is currently serving.

When the ships first collided Leading Cook Young was on HMS Fittleton's upper deck. He was making his way to the ship's galley to check for damage when there was another collision and the Fittleton capsized.

Flooding was immediate and realising that he could not escape from the forward part of the ship, he began to make his way aft. On the way he met two ratings who were both considerably shaken and confused. L/Ck Young took charge and guided them through the waist deep water to the wardroom flat from which they escaped to the surface. Before he could follow, a third rating appeared who was also unable to find an escape route so L/Ck Young stopped to assist him. He told him to take his boots off and then guided him towards the galley flat door, which on arrival they found to be closed, blocking their escape. By now there was very little air in the compartment and they were in imminent danger of drowning. He told the rating to keep close to him and swam towards the door which he managed to open; both men then escaped by swimming underwater through the wardroom flat and up to the surface.

Theft?

On the morning of the tragedy the crew of the Fittleton were paid two weeks pay in cash, approximately sixty five pounds each (worth about four hundred and twenty today). None of these wages were found on within the ship. The newspapers of the day made a big issue of this scandal blaming the Dutch salvage crew of theft. A letter to the Admiralty from a survivors MP stated that the survivor had received his wallet back but it was empty. The National Archive file has a large amount of correspondence on this issue. The Navy carried out an inquiry but concluded that if there had been theft then it was impossible to determine the culprit(s), however the survivors were reimbursed for the pay lost by the Navy.

Trader John

During a stint as Gibraltar guard ship, we went for a few days to Tangiers. Tangiers is only six kilometres from Gibraltar. On the first day that we attempted to enter the harbour, the wind was very strong and the sea was crashing against the stern and sending water across the ship. We were 'Manning the Rail'; that is the crew are lined up on each side of the ship and equally spaced apart and in full uniform. I got severely goffered[37]. The Captain gave up trying to enter the port under these conditions and we returned the following day when there was better weather.

Some of my troops and I went ashore one afternoon to a hotel, we asked whether we could use their swimming pool. To my surprise they had no objection and we spend a happy afternoon in the hotel swimming pool. As we did not use sun cream my legs got very severely sunburned. A few days later I was peeling dead skin from my thighs.

A local Trader appeared on the jetty beside our mooring selling the usual range of Moroccan souvenirs such as kaftans. One of the crew offered the trader his Navy jumper in return for a souvenir which the Trader was happy to accept. The old style Navy jumper was blue, very stiff, and very itchy. Nobody like wearing them, they were in effect just clutter. Following the initial trade members of the crew including myself traded our jumpers for souvenirs. One of our

---

[37] Goffer has 3 definitions in the RN/RM 1. A soft drink. 2. A big sea wave. 3. A punch to the mouth

lieutenants noticed what was going on and asked me what was happening, I explained that we were trading our jumpers for rabbits[38]. The lieutenant got some of his own stuff and traded for some rabbits. At the end of the day I noticed the trader wheeling away his barrow piled high with Navy jumpers, he was no doubt expecting a profitable trading day in the near future with the local Moroccans.

Lucky lad

The Navy, who seemed to be always short of technical ratings, had in 1976 recruited large numbers of radio electrical rates. There were insufficient berths on ships to place them. As such Mermaid was considerably over manned with these newly trained ratings. The ship did not have very much in the way of electronics having only two radar systems and some radio transmitter/receivers. There were no gunnery control systems, no gunnery radar and no missile systems. I had about a dozen of these ratings under my control. I tried to ensure they received as much technical experience as possible.

---

[38] Rabbit – slang for souvenir

One day a rating and I were carrying out maintenance on a radio receiver. We needed to measure the two hundred volt line and I asked the rating to measure it. I had not checked the cables of the volt meter and the wires were slightly exposed. The poor lad received a two hundred volt shock. Due to his sudden involuntary movement he banged his abdomen against the handle of the radio drawer and was in considerable pain. The sick bay medic decided to send him ashore in Copenhagen for some tests. Meanwhile the ship sailed and he was left behind.

I felt somewhat guilty about this as I was responsible for him. My guilt was somewhat assuaged after he told me what had happened in Copenhagen. He had been taken to the local hospital, been X-rayed and kept in for 24-hours for observation. He was then discharged from the hospital and the British Embassy arranged a hotel room for him. He told me he took his bag, put it in the hotel room and went to the bar. In the bar he met a girl and never went back to the hotel until it was time for him to pick up his kit and return to the ship. It was a believable story as he was an irritatingly good looking sailor and I felt a lot less guilty about the whole incident.

Hickory Dickory Dock

On a run ashore in Amsterdam one afternoon, a group of us was walking down the street when a very small mouse was spotted hopping along quite happily. One of the lads decided to chase this mouse and cornered it in a shop doorway. The mouse shot up his trouser leg so quickly that we were not aware of this until he started to shout:

"It's gone up my trousers"

He was holding one trouser leg tightly just below the knee. When we stopped laughing one of his mates removed the mouse from inside his trouser and the mouse released to live another day.

The art of the deal

Amsterdam is famous, or perhaps notorious, for a street where one can window shop for ladies of the night. In this street there are women sitting in small shop windows dressed in lingerie, knitting, reading or looking bored. These shop windows were dimly lit with red coloured lights.

One of my troops was very keen to indulge in the personal services offered by these ladies, but he was too shy to go into a shop and negotiate a deal. We walked up and down the street several times until he could summon the courage and select a lady he considered to be suitable. He and I then went inside the selected shop and I had to do the negotiating for him. Just in case the reader is wondering I did not indulge but waited outside for him to complete the transaction.

Under fire?

Luckily during my time in the Navy I was never under fire except just once. The Cod war was not a shooting war; it was rather like playing dodgems with ships.

We came up the River Thames under Tower Bridge and into the Pool of London, which is an area of the Thames between London Bridge and Tower Bridge. As we approached Tower Bridge one of the bridge crew noticed a small hole in one of port bridge windows. The bridge windows had to be able to withstand the impacts of rough seas so they were made similar way to a laminated car windscreen, but were at least three times as thick. It was then realised the hole was in fact a bullet hole and a rifle bullet was found on the floor of the bridge. During our travel up the Thames it appeared that someone had fired a rifle at us. It was presumed that it had been fired from some distance as it only had enough energy to punch a hole in the glass. I have no idea who fired the round and I don't think anybody else does. At the time the IRA[39] was active in mainland Britain so they would be the prime suspect, but no one claimed responsibility so it could have been anyone.

Fun Fact

The Royal Naval dockyard at Chatham is on the River Medway which flows into the Thames estuary. In 1944 the SS Richard Montgomery, an American liberty ship, ran aground at the confluence of the River Medway and the Thames estuary. The ships cargo was explosives. During the subsequent salvage operation to remove the cargo the ship broke her back, filled with water and sank leaving the masts protruding out of the water. Due to other concerns at the time, the ships cargo was not fully salvaged. After the war, because of fourteen hundred tons of explosives still remaining on board, it was considered to be too dangerous to salvage

---

[39] IRA – Irish Republican Army – considered by the UK to be a terrorist organisation

and the plan was, and still is, to allow the seawater to slowly rust away and dissolve the explosives. However continuing surveys have stated that any shock to or movement of the wreck could trigger the explosives. It is still there today and on our trips in and out of Chatham Dockyard we would pass by very gently.

According to a survey conducted in 2000, by the United Kingdom Maritime and Coastguard Agency, the wreck still holds munitions containing approximately 1,400 tonnes (1,500 short tons) of TNT high explosive. These comprise the following items of ordnance:

286 × 2,000 lb (910 kg) high explosive bombs
4,439 × 1,000 lb (450 kg) bombs of various types
1,925 × 500 lb (230 kg) bombs
2,815 fragmentation bombs and bomb clusters
Various explosive booster charges
Various smoke bombs, including white phosphorus bombs
Various pyrotechnic signals

Royals

HMS Mermaid was a Chatham based ship and at the time Prince Charles was a Captain in another Chatham based ship HMS Bronington. I saw him sometimes in his blue Aston Martin DB6 the same car that Prince William used on his wedding day to drive down the Mall with his new bride.

Royal Navy ratings tend to respect people on their actions rather than their position in life. Prince Charles was well thought of by Navy ratings during his service and was happy to engage with the lower deck. Prince Andrew was considered to be arrogant but Prince Phillip, the Queens consort was liked.

I am informed that Prince Phillip's helicopter landed at a Royal Navy establishment. Prince Phillip had an engagement elsewhere but the Captain met him and asked him to inspect an accommodation block. This accommodation block had been cleaned, polished and tided specifically for this inspection. However, the inspection was not scheduled on the Prince Phillips itinerary so he walked quickly to a different accommodation block and went through it without stopping. This block had not been prepared and so sailors were lying on their bunks or otherwise in an untidy manner. It is believed the Prince did this to make a point that he was not to be imposed upon.

Princess Alice, Countess of Athlone, (1883-1981) the last surviving grandchild of Queen

Victoria, visited HMS Mermaid whilst we were in London alongside HMS Belfast. She was ninety three years old but still carrying out royal duties. I noticed she had an eye for good looking sailors, so she didn't talk to me.

Entering Utopia

During the last few weeks of my time on HMS Mermaid I was promoted to Petty Officer[40] at the age of twenty four. As well as a pay rise I entered a whole new world of being a senior rate. This entitled me to three shots of spirits (each one a fifth of a gill) and two pints of beer at sea or 4 pints of beer when in port. The NAAFI[41] provided the spirits to the Petty Officers Mess. The NAAFI was only allowed to charge cost plus 10% and the spirits were duty free. Each shot (or tot) cost three pence; a mixer such as Coke would cost another five pence. This would be twenty pence and thirty two pence at 2020 values, so the prices were very cheap.

---

[40] Equivalent rank to Sergeant
[41] Navy, Army and Air Force Institutes – authorised to sell goods to servicemen

HMS London

I was drafted to HMS London in October of 1977, HMS London was a sister ship of HMS Devonshire and virtually identical except for a different number painted on the hull.

Senior Rate mess management

A Senior Rates Mess is run by a committee elected by the members. The committee consisted of President of the Mess, Treasurer, Bar Manager, and Social Secretary. These were recognised positions by the Navy. On HMS London senior rates had a mess area and a separate bunk compartment. This was useful as we were allowed to hold parties on board. To ensure success we would "conserve" our tots, not strictly allowed by the Navy, so we would have a stock available for our guests.

Bermuda wrecked

We visited Bermuda with another County class destroyer and we were moored in the old naval dockyard. The dockyard was at the far eastern end of the island, far away from Hamilton, the capital of Bermuda. Bermuda then, and now, is a beautiful place in the middle of the Atlantic. Historically Bermuda is associated with privateering, slavery and smuggling but has remained a British territory since 1615.

One incident is probably still remembered by some Bermudan residents. A stoker from our ship had a number of beers in Hamilton and decided to acquire a ride back to the dockyard. There was, in Hamilton, a mobile crane which had its jib upright and our stoker got an alcohol fuelled idea to "borrow" the crane and drive it back to the dockyard. He got it started and drove it down the main street but wrecked it into a wall at the other end. Unfortunately, with the jib upright it tore down every electrical and phone cable stretched across the main street. The Bermudan government was not pleased partly because spare parts for the crane had to be shipped from the USA. I believe the British government had to make a formal apology to Bermuda

Hurricane!

For reasons unknown to me it was decided to sail the ship through a hurricane one night, probably Hurricane Clara. In the morning (I had slept right through the night in question) I went on deck to discover that we have lost all the boats except one[42], and the Land Rover[43] which was lashed down on the flight deck. The forward Bosuns locker door had been caved in and everything in the locker had disappeared entirely. Nothing was left except for the bent door which had been punched through into the locker. The Bosuns locker contained paints, ropes, cleaning equipment and everything inside that is required to maintain the upper decks and

---

[42] we lost four out of five boats

[43] County class destroyers carried a Land Rover vehicle which was craned off when alongside and used ashore mainly by the Captain.

superstructure. The locker is situated just aft of the forward gun turret. It demonstrates just how powerful the sea can be.

Orgy, what orgy?

Following exercises in the Western Atlantic we made a Show-the-Flag visit to Philadelphia. This time we were moored at Penn's Landing the nearest jetty to the centre of Philadelphia which was about one and a quarter miles away. As previously mentioned, we were permitted to hold parties on board in our mess. The job of the Social Secretary was to issue invitations (to ladies) to such a party. When we arrived at Penn's Landing, due to some good PR by the Navy, there are a large number of reporters and TV crews on the jetty. Our Social Secretary made sure that he was the first one down the gangway. Immediately the TV Crews and reporters converged to ask him some questions. Having answered a couple of questions such as

"Do have nuclear weapons on board"

"No"

The Social Secretary ignored any further questions turned and spoke directly into the cameras and stated

"Tomorrow evening we are holding a party on board and we invite any young ladies to attend."

This invitation was broadcast across Philadelphia and as a result the following evening about eight hundred women showed up. The ship only held one hundred and twenty Senior Rates and, as mentioned before, some American women are very determined. Later accounts of the evening sounded as if an orgy had taken place. Where was I during this orgy? My friend Tom lived within walking distance of Penn's Landing and I had arranged to meet him at his apartment where we spent time putting up shelves. So I missed a major opportunity to be in attendance at a genuine orgy by helping a friend put up shelves.

One statuesque lady (who looked like Ursula Andress in the Bond movie) came on board wearing nothing except what appeared to be a string vest, a thong and sandals. She exhausted three of our toughest Petty Officers in three days.

In our mess there was a Petty Officer Chef who made some fabulous pastries. He was however very shy. He was much taken with a girl who had attached herself to a stoker Petty Officer. The chef mentioned this to the stoker who offered to trade her for three tots. The deal was done and the girl was told she was now with the chef. A few years after I had left the Navy I met the stoker in the lingerie section of Marks and Spencer's[44], it was accidental I was with my wife. He told me that the chef had married the girl, and as far as he knew, were very happy together. It was a strange coincidence to meet the stoker as this was not in a navy town.

Coincidence or message from God

During my life I have had a couple of unbelievable coincidences which I would like to recount. After I left the Navy I worked for a Johnson & Johnson company called Technicare based in Cleveland Ohio. I was at the time a specialist service engineer for gamma cameras. A Gamma camera images isotopes, which have been injected into the body and is used for the detection of cancer and other body functions such as Cardiac efficiency. Up until 1985 all the gamma camera detectors were circular with about a twenty inch diameter. In 1985 two companies released a gamma camera with a rectangular

---

[44] British department store

detector, Technicare and Toshiba. During that year I visited Cleveland to do a service course on the new Technicare rectangular camera. I travelled back by air from Cleveland and the plane was largely empty. However, a Japanese man sat next to me and I expected that after we took off he would follow the normal procedure and move to another seat. He didn't do this and remained in his seat, so I decided to talk to him. I asked him what he was doing in Cleveland and he told me he had just installed a Toshiba gamma camera with their new rectangular detector. It was the only Toshiba rectangular gamma camera in the US. I told him I just been on a course with Technicare on our rectangular camera. He was horrified because probably he believed that it had been specifically arranged for us to sit together for the purposes of industrial espionage. He stopped talking to me but he still didn't move to another seat.

Ten years later I was working for an Israeli company selling gamma cameras. I travelled with a potential customer to Israel to see a new camera but as we arrived on a Friday day we had nothing to do on the Saturday. The hotel we were staying at provided a free bus tour, probably to get us out of the hotel, and so we jumped on the tour. We went for to various sites in Jerusalem and of course that included Bethlehem. The bus dropped us at the Church of Nativity which is built on the site of the birthplace of Jesus Christ. The birth place is situated in a crypt and to access it is via a narrow medieval staircase. We were in a queue which was lined up to go down the steps. To fill the time, I related a story to my customer about an American service engineer with whom I had worked. He was a fundamentalist Baptist from Alabama with some extreme religious views. For example, he believed that Jesus only drank grape juice and not wine. As I was explaining to my customer some of the more bizarre beliefs he held, the man in front of us in the line turned around and said:

"I know that guy".

It turned out that we had both worked for Technicare although I had never met him. If it hadn't been for the first experience of coincidence, then I may have thought that it was a message from God being as we were about fifteen yards from a key religious site.

Glasgow

We visited Glasgow for some R&R. On the second night in we planned a party in the mess. Our Social Secretary had sent invitations to various hospital nurses accommodations. In the 1970s the National Health Service provided accommodation for nurses particularly those who were undergoing training. On the night in question, I recall two psychiatric nurses who came into the mess and sat down clutching their handbags and looking a little nervous. I asked them

"What would you like to drink?"

"What have you got?" We had a range of spirits such as gin, vodka, rum, whiskey and associated mixers. Alternatively, we had draught beer. One of the girls asked me how much is it. I said it's free. They replied:

"We will have a triple rum and coke". About forty nurses came to our soiree and at least half of them got absolutely hammered. We had to physically carry about a dozen girls off the ship and bribe taxi drivers to take them back to their accommodation. One of the girls went into one of the junior rates bunk spaces, which was dark, and started kissing the sailor's who were asleep. This was a highly dangerous activity as a sailor who is asleep and if he wakes up to find someone kissing them is likely to come up punchy. We dragged her out of the mess and put her in a taxi. It should be noted that even though half a dozen of the girls had passed out we were perfect gentleman.

Furry friend?

One Sunday evening I returned from weekend leave and prepared to get into my bunk. The bunk space was very dark and as I levered myself into the bunk, I discovered there was something large and furry tickling my feet. I sprang out of my bunk to investigate, it turned out that it was the bear skin fur cap of a Guardsman. I learnt that we were to visit Poland and we were to take with us a band made up from the five regiments of the Guards. The Guards regiment is the one who wears red tunics and bear skin fur hats. They are seen in London guarding Buckingham Palace and the Tower of London. We took with us to Poland the band which included Scottish bag pipers. The band was commanded by an officer whose uniform included a sword which, as he would normally ride a horse, was slung low. Normally the sword would drag on the ground if on foot. Following complaints from the upper deck maintenance team the ships Carpenter fitted the end of his scabbard with a small wooden wheel so that it would not scrape the deck.

Navy Officer? Gentleman? No!

Royal Navy officers are obliged to carry their swords by decree of Queen Victoria who was shocked to hear that Navy Officers had lied to mutineers. The Queen stated that Royal Navy officers were not gentlemen. The decree was to last for one hundred years but has not yet been rescinded.

Gdynia

Our trip to Poland was to the port of Gdynia, this was to be the first official visit of a British warship since the Second World War. We were given shore leave but we had to wear uniform. Every day the Guards band would play and march up and down in the main square, but nobody had told the locals of our visit. The few people watching this parade were astonished to see a brightly coloured British military band marching and playing. The local dogs went bonkers because the bearskins are made form real bears. I saw three dogs chasing the band, barking loudly and snapping at the bandsmen ankles. The visit was during the communist rule and my view of Gdynia was that it was a fairly drab place. It had been totally rebuilt since the

Second World War as the German and Soviet armies had devastated the town destroying ninety percent of the buildings.

One afternoon my run ashore oppo[45] and I met a Scottish bandsman who seem to be about to suffer a mental breakdown. He was wearing a uniform which included tartan trousers and a Glengarry hat. The local people were looking at him surprised to see someone in such an outré outfit and he seemed to be suffering from stage fright. We escorted him to an area with fewer people until he felt better.

Our uniform as a Petty Officer consisted of black suit, white shirt with black tie, and with gold badges on the arms. We were not that different from Polish officers in terms of uniform. We went into a cafe for a coffee and were surprised when a girl of about nine years old left her mother's table, carried her ice cream dish and sat with us on our table. I don't know why she decided to sit with us, we said hello, but she just smiled at us and kept eating her ice-cream. We were not able to find out why she came and sat with us as neither she nor her mother spoke English.

---

[45] Oppo – Navy slang describing a friend from work

Perhaps another example of all the nice girls love a sailor.

Later that evening we went into a nightclub which had a fifties style but with a lino floor and light weight cafe furniture. We had just sat down at a table when two girls in their early twenties, who had obviously been sampling far too much vodka, literally threw themselves at us. My oppo and I went over backwards and all four of us ended up in a big heap on the floor. We were just trying to have a quiet beer. After we had extracted ourselves from the girls and set up the furniture again, we were approached by a Polish man. He lent on the table and gabbled a whole lot of Polish at us in a loud voice. He was obviously very drunk and after a couple of minutes he slowly sank to the floor and was taken away way by his friends. So much for a quiet drink and maintaining decorum.

Cocktails Navy fashion

Our visit to Gdynia was part of a PR exercise and we were ordered to hold a cocktail party. A number of Polish Navy senior rates were invited plus their wives. The Navy approach to making a cocktail was to fill a two pint water jug with gin and tonic and a few lumps of ice. The gin and tonic was about four parts gin and one part tonic. The Poles, who were substantial drinkers, consumed vast quantities and became quite merry. At the end of the party, they seemed disinclined to leave and go home so we called in one of the Scottish pipers and play his bagpipes. When the pipes are played indoors, they peak at one hundred and sixteen decibels about as loud as a chainsaw. The Scots have used bagpipes as a psychological weapon of war for hundreds of years as they can be heard for several miles. They were effective on our guests who left shortly after the Piper started to play.

Dangerous Vodka

It was possible to buy Polish Vodka at eighty percent by volume which is over one hundred and fifty percent proof. It is dangerous to drink and is inflammable as well as being illegal to sell in the UK. Gdynia had numerous Vodka bars which sold only Vodka and some mixers. Unfortunately, some of our junior rates were not aware of its dangers and one lad gave himself alcoholic poisoning by drinking too much too quickly. He was lucky to survive.

Hi Ho, Hi Ho

On our return to the UK from Poland a group from our ship were invited to dinner in the Guards Regiment Sergeant's Mess in Aldershot. The Guards Regiment is possibly the most formal of the British Army. I did not attend this dinner as at the time I was on leave; however, this is the tale I heard on my return to the ship.

The dinner had gone well with large amounts of alcohol consumed and after dinner the contingent of sailors decided to enact one of the traditional navy entertainments. This is called Snow White and the Seven Dwarfs. It is designed to entertain the locals and goes down well in such places as North America and other English-speaking countries. First of all seven people go outside the bar and the eighth man orders seven beers. These are lined up on the bar and when they are ready, he shouts 'Hi Ho'. From outside the bar comes up answering shout of 'Hi Ho'. The door opens and the seven ratings enter marching in line on their knees with their right hand on the shoulder of rating in front simultaneously singing the classic Walt Disney song 'Hi ho Hi ho and off to work we go'. They shuffle to the bar still on their knees and each one takes a beer and drinks it in one. However, about the time that the 'dwarfs' were marching on their knees to the bar, the Army Duty Officer entered the mess to see what all the noise was about. He was totally shocked by the apparent chaos going on and said to one of the ratings who was watching:

"I am going to report this appalling behaviour to your senior officer".

The rating replied, "That will be Dwarf number three sir, he's our Commander"[46]. At which point the Duty Officer left.

Stand still training

In the autumn of that year, I was bragging in the mess to the Gunnery Petty Officer about how much experience I had had in drill and marching, particularly as I had spent almost four years in the Air Training Corps[47]. I have to admit that in terms of drill I was pretty useless, not quite as bad as Corporal Jones in Dad's Army[48], but getting pretty close. As a result of my bragging the Gunnery Petty Officer, who was responsible for drill training, put me down

---

[46] Equivalent to Lieutenant Colonel
[47] A cadet force for 13-18 year olds
[48] British Sitcom about the Home Guard in WW2

for the to be a member of the Royal Guard for Remembrance Sunday. The Remembrance Day event is held at the Cenotaph[49] in London every year in November to remember those who died in war. It is normally attended by the Queen, hence the Royal Guard. The Royal Guard trains for three weeks before Remembrance Sunday and includes marching in the Lord Mayor's parade as well as being at the Cenotaph. A large part of the training is called 'Stand still training'. This is to acclimatise the Guard to the one hour of standing still at the Cenotaph. The Guard is required to stand still without perceptively moving. It is especially focused on keeping the head still. Standing still is a lot harder than it sounds. Try standing still without moving for ten minutes. It can be an entertaining game to play with the children at Christmas. It is particularly difficult to stand still for an hour. At the end of the hour, it feels as if it is impossible to make muscles obey the brain. I did about a week of the training before I was rumbled as being useless at drill, so I was sent home on leave. A total winner for me to get two weeks leave but it does give me sympathy for the guard standing still at the Cenotaph

---

[49] The Cenotaph – tomb of the unknown soldier representing those killed in WW1.

during the memorial service. I now look closely at the televised event to see if the Royal Guard moves their heads. As the sailors wear white hats it is very noticeable if they move.

This is the science bit.

On HMS London, my role was the maintenance of the gunnery radar and associated control systems for the two gun turrets. The radar set was about the size of a microwave; there's not that much difference between a radar set and a microwave as they both work on the same principles. The radar was made by Plessey and was new, using microprocessors and thyristors. As the County Class destroyers had originally been designed in the 1950s the control amplifiers used valves such as pentodes. These amplifiers took the signal from the radar and other sources and sent it to the turrets to control the guns. The amplifiers were prone to drift and needed daily tuning.

Naval gunnery is a complex affair; calculations have to be made for target movement and direction, the movement of the ship, the amount of energy in the cordite, the internal diameter of the gun barrels, and the direction and speed of travel of the ship. The rotation of the Earth also has to be compensated by setting the latitude of the ship's position. All these factors have to be calculated in real time. The complete system has to be tuned so that the guns will hit the target.

The anti aircraft target we used was one towed by an aircraft on a very long cable. We spent a month in Gibraltar training Warfare officers in gun control. Every morning I got up at five o'clock, tested and tuned the system ready to start exercises at about eight o'clock. We would spend the day firing the guns at the air towed target. We would finish at about four in the afternoon and then I would assist in preparing the telemetry results to be sent to the Admiralty often finishing at about nine o'clock in evening.

The whole gunnery system worked well and occasionally we would fire at a radio-controlled surface target. This consisted of a twenty five foot boat which was capable of doing about ten knots. The launch controllers were very unhappy when we put two shells (non explosive) through their boat. Normally it is very difficult to hit a fast-moving surface target as often radar would be confused by the waves generating false readings known as 'clutter'.

Every time the guns fire the internal surface of the barrel is worn away very slightly. There is an automatic adjustment which takes this into account. This wear on the internal diameter of the barrel reduces that muzzle velocity. During the training period we fired over two thousand rounds and the guns were worn beyond our ability to compensate for the wear.

Toilets flushed by the guns

A minor problem was that when the 4.5 inch guns fire it causes a shock wave through the fabric of the ship. This shock wave would trigger the forward junior rates heads[50] causing them to flush. The toilet flush water was supplied from the fire main. With all the toilets flushing at once, the fire main pump would lose pressure and an alarm would sound. To counter this effect the forward heads would be closed during firing.

---

[50] Heads – naval term for toilets

HMS Collingwood

I returned to Collingwood in 1978 to be an instructor on the 909 missile radar control system. The system was built by Marconi and was fitted on the type 42 destroyers. The control systems were housed in eight six foot high cabinets. They were filled with racks of printed circuit boards slightly smaller than an A4 sheet of paper. The system was unreliable and the sailors who tried to maintain it and keep them it running were working twelve to fourteen hour days.

It had a fundamental design flaw. A circuit board has components on one side and circuit strips on the other side. The two are connected through holes in the board and the component wires are threaded through and soldered to the circuits. In the 909 Radar, for some unknown reason, each hole through a circuit board had a steel rivet. This produced a meeting of metals of copper, steel, lead and tin. Each of these metals expands and contracts at different rates as they heat up and cool down. The effect of this was to create a 'dry joint'. A dry joint is a micro crack which prevents electrical conductivity but is often invisible to the naked eye. Ships equipped with the 909 Radar frequently employed a rating whose sole job was to solder the printed circuit boards to resolve this issue of 'dry joints'.

There was a bank of about one hundred lights each of which was supposed to illuminate in the event of a fault. I was informed that the record for the least about of illuminated lights was fourteen.

Another issue was the Marconi policy towards their design engineers. When talking to one I was informed that Marconi would recruit engineers from university but would not provide them with any further technical training. In order to learn about the latest microchips and devices when designing improvements to the system the engineers would use one of the latest devices in the upgrade. The effect of this was that the system had all kinds of microchips, transistors and diodes installed. To be fair to Marconi the UK government had rushed the 909 radar system into service before it had been properly developed. The combination of all of this was that the estimated mean time between failures it was about twenty minutes.

A Chief Petty Officer, who was an instructor on the system, had been removed from his ship for medical reasons caused by the pressure of trying to keep the radar system running. The major components of the radar, such as the magnetron, were situated in the centre of the compartment containing the printed circuit racks. These units ran at very high voltages. One day we wanted to measure the current in the 18000 volt line with an AVO 8 meter. This is an electrical mechanical device and when we switched on the system found the needle swung in the wrong direction. We needed to reverse the polarity. As we were unable to contact Dr Who and borrow a sonic screwdriver we would have to do this via mechanical button on the AVO. I was looking around for a wooden broom handle with which to press the button when I heard a loud bang. The Chief had decided to press the button with his finger. The 18000 Volts arced within the AVO and gave the Chief an electric shock which threw him across the room. Luckily, he was only shaken but not hurt; this did not help his medical condition.

In 1980 I was promoted to Chief Petty Officer[51]. By this time I had decided to leave

---

[51] Rank equivalent to Colour Sergeant

the Navy and had put in my resignation. On 2nd February 1981 I left the Royal Navy. I left for a number of reasons. I was married with a lovely daughter and the wine, women and song stuff had become tedious. I had also lost confidence in the management after the Fittleton affair. My thinking was that I was young enough to start a new career (I was twenty eight) particularly now I had some technical skills.

Submarines? No thank you!

Any one in the Royal Navy can volunteer for service in submarines. Ratings received extra pay for being a submariner. In 1976 this was about £100 per month worth about £750 per month today.

I didn't fancy being a submariner because I really didn't want to do the 'tank'. Part of the compulsory training for submariners is to qualify in the 'tank'. The 'tank' was a ninety foot vertical tank filled with water. The potential submariner entered a compartment at the bottom which was then flooded with water from the vertical tank. Once the pressure had equalised the submariner would then enter the bottom of the vertical tank via a hatch and swim to the top. This is done without any breathing apparatus.

The other issue is the conditions, especially on the diesel powered submarines. Space is at a premium and washing seemed to be optional unlike on surface vessels. Some submarines were reputed to have 'hot bunking' that is where one rating gets out of the bunk and the next one immediately gets in.

The joke at that time was

Question: "What is the difference between a submariner and a Hells Angel?"

Answer: "The Hells Angel wears a uniform."

Nuclear submarines have a better environment and now the Navy allows women to serve I'm sure improvements will follow.

Life after the Navy

What did the Navy do for me?

I was never 'anchor faced' as they call it and my character tends towards being somewhat laid back (Idle). Did I enjoy my time? Not really, the life, particularly on ships, was ninety-seven percent boredom and three percent excitement.

Within the Navy I felt I was outside the normal social class system. One of the benefits of this is that respect for others is based on their actions and not on their position in life.

I did gain a lot of confidence and technical skills. The Navy also provides a perspective on life which has carried me through some interesting times. When in doubt be bold and never refuse a challenge. Here is an example.

Serious sauna

In 1986 I was working at my first sales job. My role was to find international agents for the company's products. I found an agent in

Finland and was invited by his company to visit and carry out product demonstrations to potential customers. Early one morning I flew to Helsinki, and on arrival, met the agent and his sales manager. I carried out the demonstrations to a group of customers and afterward the agent was very pleased and offered to take me to his sauna club as a treat. I had to wait until the following day for a return flight and, as I had nothing better to do, agreed.

We arrived at the sauna club at about noon. The club was housed in a traditional wooden building in a forest. We entered and the agent paid the fees to the receptionist. I was then informed that the club was men only but it wasn't a gay club. All the staff were female but it wasn't like that either. We went into the changing room where the agent told me to take off all my clothes. At this point I would like to emphasize that I had only known these two men for about two hours. I applied the maxim of when in doubt, be bold. So I took off all my clothes and as they say 'let it all hang out'. The agent gave me a face flannel and I wondered what I was going to do with a one foot square piece of towelling. I slung it, in a nonchalant manner, over my shoulder.

The agent said "follow me Nick" and we went into a sauna. This was about twelve feet square and had a set of stacked benches with some higher than the other. It was hot! I think it was in excess of one hundred and eighty degrees Fahrenheit. I sat on the lowest bench hoping it would be slightly cooler. There were a number of Finns already ensconced, some of whom were gently beating themselves with birch twigs. I tried the twigs, but I would not recommend them as it breaks up the slightly cooler air beside the skin and its feels as if the twigs are red hot.

After ten minutes I realised that I either had to run for the door or pass out. The agent saw that I was suffering and we left the sauna and went through another door. I stepped through the door and was enveloped in steam and could not see a thing.

As the steam cleared I saw that I was now outside the building. It was February and the temperature was fourteen degrees Fahrenheit (minus ten degrees Celsius) with snow on the ground. The 'steam' was coming from my sweat and as I looked around I could see Finns lying on the snow, chatting and smoking, whilst totally naked.

The agent said, 'follow me Nick' and we walked down a path onto a snow covered lawn. The path stopped in the middle of the lawn and I then saw it was not a lawn it was frozen sea. The ice was about six inches thick which I could see because some fool had chopped a big hole in it about twelve feet in diameter. The agent and the sales manager jumped in and beckoned to me to do the same. I have to admit I bottled out. My thinking was that these men had been doing this for years, but if I jumped in the shock may stop my heart.

There was another issue. The sweat was running down my legs and freezing my feet to the jetty. In order to prevent this, I had to march on the spot. Whilst the agent was swimming around, I heard the noise of traffic. I turned to my right and thirty yards away was a main highway out of Helsinki with heavy traffic. Although it was a clear day there was nothing to see as my male external protuberances had disappeared due to the cold.

We went back inside and tried various types of sauna such as hot and smoky, hot and hot and hot and humid, the last one being the worst. In between we took showers.

Eventually the agent suggested that we have a coffee. We went into a café area and the agent bought three coffees from the lady behind the counter. (She was fully dressed, we were still naked) I hope the agent had a tab as I don't where he could be hiding his money. In the middle of the room was a large log fire above which there was a trumpet style chimney. The agent suggested that we all sit round the fire. There was a small problem with this fire as it was fuelled by frozen pine logs and as the resin heated up it spat it at us. The resin was also alight. So I was sitting naked with a hot cup of coffee above my more delicate parts whilst trying to dodge the fiery shots coming from the logs.

The sales manager was the hairiest man I've ever seen. It looked as if he was wearing a gorilla suit but without the head. As the resin landed on him his hair was catching fire but he casually extinguished the small fires on his legs by patting them with his hand.

All the time this was going on we kept up polite conversation as if nothing untoward was happening. The agent kept up a stream of terrible jokes a couple of which I still remember so here they are.

'Brezhnev, the Russian soviet leader went to East Germany on an official visit. In the evening he travelled back by train. The train stopped at a station and his aide asked him 'where are we?' Brezhnev put his hand out of the window and said 'we are in East Germany'. Later the train stopped at another station. Same question, Brezhnev put his hand out of the window and said, 'we are in Poland'. Some time later the train stopped at another station, same question so Brezhnev put his hand out of the window and said, 'we are in mother Russia'. His aide asked, 'how you know where you are just by putting your hand out the window'. Brezhnev replied, 'at the first station they kissed my hand, in the second station they spat on my hand but at the third station they stole my watch.'

'What is the difference between Heaven and Hell? In Heaven there is an English policeman, a French chef, an Italian lover and the whole place is run by Germans. In Hell there is a English cook, a French policeman, a German lover and the whole place is run by Italians.'

After we had drunk our coffee the agent said, 'Nick I've booked you a wash'. I was led into a large white tiled room in the middle of which was a stout wooden bench over which a rubber sheet was spread. Beside the bench was a large Finnish lady. It was indicated to me to lie on the rubber sheet. The lady then put on a glove which was made of Scotch -Brite (the sort of material used for cleaning pots and pans), rubbed on a large bar of soap and then vigorously applied the glove to my body. There was a queue of men waiting for this treatment, so she was not hanging about. I was told to flip, and the other side of my body was suitably scrubbed. Beside the lady was a large barrel of cold water and a bucket, this she used to sluice me down and wash off the soap. The whole process took about four minutes.

I got up and left and as I looked at my body every single lump or bump on my skin was gone and there were little pinpricks of blood everywhere. I have never felt so clean in my entire life.

About the author

Nick was born in Brighton then moved to Eastbourne when he was about one year old. He went to school in Eastbourne and left Eastbourne Grammar School with a small clutch of 'O' levels. He served in the Royal Navy from 1971 to 1980 after which he went into sales and marketing of medical imaging equipment. He is now retired and living in Surrey.

© Nicholas Collett JP
www.nfcol.org

www.ingramcontent.com/pod-product-compliance
Lightning Source LLC
LaVergne TN
LVHW010316070426
835513LV00021B/2404